Emotionally unavailable

Elena Watkiss

Emotionally unavailable © 2022 Elena Watkiss

All rights reserved.

No part of this publication may be reproduced, stored in a retrieval system, or transmitted, in any form or by any means, electronic, mechanical, photocopying, recording or otherwise, without the prior written permission of the presenters.

Elena Watkiss asserts the moral right to be identified as author of this work.

Presentation by *BookLeaf Publishing*

Web: www.bookleafpub.com

E-mail: info@bookleafpub.com

ISBN: 9789357690522

First edition 2022

This is dedicated to my late parents, John and Lorraine. x

ACKNOWLEDGEMENT

Thank you to my friend for recommending to me that I do this! Hopefully it's not a complete disaster.

PREFACE

When I write poetry I write because it helps me to express emotions that I would normally not be able to express. This is the closest thing I have come to publishing a personal diary without publishing my actual diary.

Bravery

I see all of you with so much strength,
Soldiers of soul mercy.
Where I feel
My growing pains,
Will be the death of me.

Infancy

Once there was home,
Painted white
And painted too
By nature's undiminished effect
Of ware on man made things.

However the house wasn't tired,
In fact its character proceeded itself.
Its foundations lay tucked away
Behind apricot coloured roses,
And its dark green bushes
That grew without strain
Adorning the house
Like a blanket being lain
On sleeping child.

Protective, loving and yielding.
There are trees surrounding the house
The height reaching the second floor.

Which when the sun shone its rays behind the trees,
It casts dappled golden sun light
On the sheer white of the houses' exterior
Like drops of honey with milk.

When a gentle wind blows
It moves the soft and delicate leaves
Swaying back and forth
Creating hypnotic shadows
moving in attuned rhythm.

Empower

Her shiny skin
Like silk
Her heart sings
Her worth
Her body
Breaks jeans
Her body
Breaks seams
She wears her own clothes
Man made things
Do not touch
Her
Ethe-real-ness

Windows to The Soul

The house stands there
but nobody's home,
A small girl cries in the night
but she is all alone.
They say your eyes are the windows to
Your soul,

The owners left there,
The calendar hanging perfectly
On the wall
Frozen
In 1984.
Not a warm hand
To turn it.

The house had its inhabitants
Oh yes,

They remained anonymous
For quite some time
Until they
Appeared
At night
Otherworldly
And strange

She didn't know what to make of them
Until..
At a later age.

She had been told ghost stories
Before,
She knew of disembodied voices
Shuffles on the floor
And knocks
From a strange man,
All the familiar
On her door.

'Leave me alone!'
She wish she could cry,
But she was frozen
Not even a blink of an eye.

So the house stands there
Still,
However
As the years pass
Nature,
It begins
Its all encompassing
Journey
Its elegant vines,
Adorned with emerald leaves
That shine brightly in the sun.

Colours

Life isn't black and white.
Not only is there grey,
But there are colours
That you can't even imagine.
You can let that be restricting,
Or you can let that be incredibly liberating
We are the product of that.

Ease

In a world
And a time
that craves ease,
We must accept
The dark when it comes.
And if you can fully accept the dark
For all that it brings
And all its messages,
The light will flood your heart, mind and body.
And darkness will become
A familiar friend.

To those

Are my emotions to available?
Are they too loud?
Too brash?
Do they scream and rattle you?
Your emotions are only present
Only when you think
To be a woman means to be silent and
Soft
To be woman means to be forever young
And to be a spark in a man's eye
To be a slave and never dare to be
Brave
To be an object you adorn on your
Finger
And to never move or change
To stay small and ensure our minds never know
Its own worth
To keep our minds in captivity
I can tell you
We are more
To be a woman
Is to scream!
To be a woman
Is to be seen!
And never touched

Without her
Sacred permission!
To be a woman
Is to be larger than life!
To be a woman
Means to thrive
And this goes
Out to all those
Who have been
Deprived
Stuck
And blinded
To themselves
Because something was
Blocking your light.

You are blind
For a short time
Because
Your soul
Is beyond bright.

Riches and rags.

Her eyes glitter
In the cameras flash
She's glamorous
All the men are a catch
Her life's
A moving picture but she's too,
Afraid they'll ditch her.
Drugs mix in her veins
And it's all in the name
Of fame.

It keeps her awake,
It keeps her peppy,
It keeps the weight
Where it should be.

Hazy chiffon day dream,
She sees herself in broken glass.

Tears pave a steady stream
Down her cheeks.

An infant on her mind.

However,
Shes been wined and dined
What feels a thousand times.
So for now she stays within
The pines.

A beauty surrounded by diamonds
Where no one can find her.

The bubbles in her champagne glass still fizzing.

Youth

I miss the loose dust
Felt underneath my toes.

Although scraping my wounds
Peace was there,

Old wire scrapes my shins
That's the thing with sins.

Dark chasm,
I still feel the feathers
Of that time.

Myself

There comes a time
In modern day,
When ones persona
Becomes as flat as their face.

On that screen
Where the image of themselves is that of one
That must be up kept.

So their face is kept flat,
And the rest of them sinks down into the
Murky depths of pretension.

Their necks stretching so high as that they may still,
Look down on everyone else,

Only to realise their head is just above water.

Opinions

We tie our identity to our opinions,
We give them weight and give over our
Control and sanity to them.

We build walls because of our opinions
and set out to destroy others.

"An opinion different from mine must be a
threat and I must fight it!"
With the invisible weapons and invisible
shields.

Opinions have become commercialised.
Some sell ... some don't.

They've become steel and unmovable and they
lodge themselves in your side.

Making your blind spots blinder
The people yell "There must be a wrong
and the must be a right! And I am always on the
right side!"

Justice doesn't exist in this realm.
You cannot find justice in opinions.

Opinions shouldn't be words of steel and Weight
But rather tools to the beginning of
Honest, grown up communication.

You can find justice in truth, clarity and unbiased thought,
Something that has been starved from our society.

But that is just my opinion.

Social Anxiety

My fear keeps me far from them
But
My heart doth yearn
For the warmth of their company
And its burn...

Forgiveness

Forgive those
That have hurt you
In the past.

For the pain is not for you to keep
Even if the valley
Of the scar doth run deep.

To hold on until the bitter end
Your pain shall never amend.

Change

I've changed
but nothing has changed at all,
The surface of pain
Has cracked and crumbled
But now I see the well
My conscious has bared
And gave birth to.

The depth as unknown.
Primal thoughts once our friends,
Now our enemies.

In the modern world
I no longer fight beasts
Just the ones in my mind
Biting my skin until bleeds,
As sometimes I feel trapped in a cage.
Animals revenge.

Expansiveness of the now is breath taking
But please don't try to take my breath away
For now I live here.

Freedom

Wild human,
Your are free.

You have no money
Yet the government
Seem to still ask
They even took your shoes.

Your a living by product
Of corrupt system
That can barely support
You.

Father clock and china doll

Father clock and China doll,
The memory of it all
Haunts me in the small hours
That I might find you.

Amongst the dark heavy green trees,
Strewn with dew and cob webs,
That look like diamond necklaces.
Somewhere in there I find myself too.

I lay peaceful,
Face of porcelain
And I listen to chimes and ticks
Of father clock.

Codependance

I want to huddle to you so close,
So as that we are one.

Maybe I'll just be using you
As a human jacket.

So that I can feel warm and safe
Not to sound like a cannibal.

But sometimes it rubs off on you
When you have been their food for so long.
I want someone to stick a dummy
In my mouth, and tell me lies
Of shiny cars and lots of money
Feeling infantile and stupid.

Connectivity

Machines can't see
What we see.

Yet we fervently
Want to see through machines
Eyes,
Digitised and detached.

Pixels hurt
Building blocks to a false sense of security,
And connectivity.

Yet we all know it
It seems like we all know we are getting duped.
However we will still go along with it.

Because maybe... hopefully
We will get invited to that party
With the golden men, cold and stiff.
What happened to blood and flesh
The feel of air on your skin
And dirt between your toes.
Your hands and mind harmonising
The only real connectivity.

We no longer connect to ourselves
Can we really be expected
To connect with each other?

Hate

I never,
Want to be
So hateful,
That
I am blind to kindness.
However if cancer
Had a face
I'd punch it.

Time

Old smells and
Velvet jackets,
A slight breeze and
Clear starry nights,
Far away tales being told
Under waves of blankets,
Perhaps a shipwrecked pirate
Or maybe a ghost.

Dreamt

All along I was dreaming,
Of wide open spaces.

Friendly faces.

Deserts with horizons that were never met,
Oceans that hugged the curve of our earth.

Without all the pain of it,
Wishing time could stand still.

All this longing,
Believing I wasn't big or tall enough
Too reach out...

Milton Keynes UK
Ingram Content Group UK Ltd.
UKHW020740291223
435170UK00015B/636